Resting In God's Infinity And A

Message To The Spiritually

Discouraged

Leslie D. Weatherhead

Kessinger Publishing's Rare Reprints

Thousands of Scarce and Hard-to-Find Books on These and other Subjects!

- Americana
- Ancient Mysteries
- Animals
- Anthropology
- Architecture
- Arts
- Astrology
- Bibliographies
- Biographies & Memoirs
- Body, Mind & Spirit
- Business & Investing
- Children & Young Adult
- Collectibles
- Comparative Religions
- Crafts & Hobbies
- Earth Sciences
- Education
- Ephemera
- Fiction
- Folklore
- Geography
- Health & Diet
- History
- Hobbies & Leisure
- Humor
- Illustrated Books
- Language & Culture
- Law
- Life Sciences
- Literature
- Medicine & Pharmacy
- Metaphysical
- Music
- Mystery & Crime
- Mythology
- Natural History
- Outdoor & Nature
- Philosophy
- Poetry
- Political Science
- Science
- Psychiatry & Psychology
- Reference
- Religion & Spiritualism
- Rhetoric
- Sacred Books
- Science Fiction
- Science & Technology
- Self-Help
- Social Sciences
- Symbolism
- Theatre & Drama
- Theology
- Travel & Explorations
- War & Military
- Women
- Yoga
- *Plus Much More!*

We kindly invite you to view our catalog list at:
http://www.kessinger.net

RESTING IN GOD'S INFINITY

THE AIM OF THIS SERMON IS TO HELP US TO REALIZE A LITTLE MORE truly how great God is and, therefore, how adequate he is for any situation that can arise in our own lives or in the world. As we do this, we can rest our minds and hearts in his infinity.

It has been very hard to choose a text because there are so many. Let me give you some of them:

> As the heavens are higher than the earth, so are my ways higher than your ways, and my thought than your thoughts. —Isa. 55:9

> Let all those that seek thee rejoice and be glad in thee: let such as love thy salvation say continually, The Lord be magnified. But I am poor and needy; yet the Lord thinketh upon me. —Ps. 40:16-17

> O magnify the Lord with me, and let us exalt his name together. I sought the Lord, and he heard me, and delivered me from all my fears.
> —Ps. 34:3-4

I should like to add to these passages others from poets who did not live in time to have their words included in the Bible. I hope it will not hurt anybody's feelings if I say that the inspiration of the Bible is not essentially different in kind from the inspiration of religious poets and prophets of later periods. Do you know this passage from Sidney Lanier's great poem "The Marshes of Glynn"?

> As the marsh-hen secretly builds on the watery sod,
> Behold I will build me a nest on the greatness of God:
> I will fly in the greatness of God as the marsh-hen flies
> In the freedom that fills all the space 'twixt the marsh and the skies:
> By so many roots as the marsh-grass sends in the sod
> I will heartily lay me a-hold on the greatness of God:
> Oh, like to the greatness of God is the greatness within
> The range of the marshes, the liberal marshes of Glynn.

And, finally, two lines from Elizabeth Barrett Browning's poem "The Rhyme of the Duchess May":

> And I smiled to think God's greatness flowed around our
> incompleteness,—
> Round our restlessness, his rest.

So much for texts!

I wonder if you have ever noticed that no biblical poet or prophet sets the thought of God's greatness over against the thought of man's littleness in order to make man feel insignificant and of no consequence. On the contrary, all the great biblical writers set the thought of God's greatness over against the need of man. They magnify God not to make man feel small, but to make man feel that the resources of this mighty Being are at his disposal. We are not to argue, "If he is so great, I must be of no account at all," but rather, "How great he is, and therefore how able to take care of me and look after my interests."

I should be interested if any can find a passage which denies this. Even in that magnificent passage in the fortieth chapter of Isaiah, where the prophet is rejoicing in the might of God, I claim that this point is not denied. We read of God that he "comprehended the dust of the earth in a measure, and weighed the mountains in scales, and the hills in a balance"; that to him the "nations are as a drop of a bucket," and "the small dust of the balance"; and that "he taketh up the isles as a very little thing." But the passage is introduced by the verse: "He shall feed his flock like a shepherd: he shall gather the lambs with his arm, and carry them in his bosom." And the mighty passage ends with the words: "They that wait upon the Lord shall renew their strength; they shall mount up with wings as eagles; they shall run, and not be weary; and they shall walk, and not faint." In other words, this mighty God, whom it is absurd for the maker of idols to try to imprison in a piece of wood or metal, is one whose vast energies are at the disposal of those who trust in him.

Or take that other passage, in Psalm 8, which might seem to dispute my claim. The psalmist says: "When I consider thy heavens, the work of thy fingers, the moon and the stars, which thou hast ordained; what is man, that thou art mindful of him? and the son of man, that thou visitest him?" But don't stop there! For the poet goes on to say: "Thou hast made him a little lower than God"—in the original we have the word God (*elohim*), not angels—"and hast crowned him with glory and honor. . . . Thou hast put all things under his feet." In other words, the poet is rejoicing in the glory of God in order that he may rest the minds of men in God's infinity.

In Psalm 147 we have a similar adjacency of ideas: "He healeth the broken in heart. and bindeth up their wounds. He telleth the number of the stars; he calleth them all by their names."

The psalmists never seem to think of the greatness of God without reveling in the thought of what that means in terms of man's comfort and strengthening.

In Psalm 34—the text already given—the psalmist cries out: "O magnify the Lord with me, and let us exalt his name together," and immediately goes on to say: "*I* sought the Lord, and he heard me. . . . *They* looked unto him, and were lightened." And then. most marvelous of all, "This poor man cried, and the Lord heard *him,* and saved him out of all his troubles." And remember that when the psalmist cries out, as he so often does, "O magnify the Lord," he does not mean, "Let us tell God what a wonderful person he is, and let us in our insignificance crawl at his feet." He means, "Let us realize how big God is and how adequate for all our needs, and let us rest our minds and hearts, our worries, our concern for our loved ones, our whole nation's troubles, on his breast."

Behold I will build me a nest on the greatness of God.

I am rather jealous for religion in this matter because so often it seems as though the scientist, the poet, the musician, and the dramatist point to a bigger God than ours. I would commend to you the reading of Samuel Foss's great poem "Two Gods." Let me quote two stanzas only:

As wider skies broke on his view,
God greatened in his growing mind;
Each year he dreamed his God anew,
And left his older God behind.

> He saw the boundless scheme dilate,
> In star and blossom, sky and clod;
> And as the universe grew great,
> He dreamed for it a greater God.[1]

It is that greater God that so many of us need. And the scientist, whom some may think of as undermining our faith in God, is really a servant of God pointing to the vastness of the Creator.

I am not going to bring to you scientific facts and quote astronomical figures about the vast distance between one star and another or the insignificance of this planet compared with the size and weight of others. (As Pascal said, *"Le silence éternal de ces espaces infinis m'effraie."*) But you remember how Kepler, the astronomer, cried out after much study of the heavens, "O God, I am thinking thy thoughts after thee." If the Milky Way is one of his ideas, what kind of God is this? How, in the light of such a thought, we can hear the intensity of the Master's voice crying, "O men, how little you trust him!" (Matt. 6:30—Moffatt.) Jeans and Eddington and Whitehead have all taught us to have a greater God. Toward the end of Jeans's book *The Mysterious Universe* we find this: "The stream of knowledge is heading towards a non-mechanical reality: the universe begins to look more like a great thought than like a great machine." Popular astronomy is teaching us all to "think God's thoughts after him."

Then think how the poet laments the littleness of religion. Like the scientist, his own God seems bigger than ours. I cannot avoid the feeling that that was in Wordsworth's mind when so passionately he cried:

> We have given our hearts away, a sordid boon!
>
> .   .   .   .
>
> Great God! I'd rather be
> A Pagan suckled in a creed outworn;
> So might I, standing on this pleasant lea,
> Have glimpses that would make me less forlorn;
> Have sight of Proteus rising from the sea;
> Or hear old Triton blow his wreathèd horn.

[1] *Songs of the Average Man.* By permission of Lothrop, Lee & Shepard Co.

Surely he means that we have whittled down our religion—a religion that should lift us to tuneful harmony with the whole universe —until it has become a triviality.

Or, if you love music and have listened to Bach's "Toccata and Fugue in D minor" or Liszt's "Hungarian Rhapsody"—both of them, you remember, opening in the same way with a series of majestic phrases—I imagine that your heart has been singing, "How great is God, for he is the source of all beauty!"

The dramatist, too, gives one the same feeling. Do you remember near the end of Bernard Shaw's *St. Joan* how Joan lifts up her arms to heaven and cries, "When will the earth be ready to receive thy saints? How long, O Lord, how long?" For myself, I wish Shaw had finished the play at that point. To me everything else *is* anticlimax. But did you not get in that play the sense of the long, slow processes of life moving out in the hands of a patient God to an end which no man could deny, working through pain and suffering and frustration to some majestic climax beyond all the dreams of man?

And then put over against all that—the revelation of God which the scientist, the poet, the musician, and the dramatist make—put over against that, I say, the conception of religion which you get from so many religious people. It seems trivial, fussy, petty, little-minded, gossipy. Mind! I know the actors quarrel among themselves, and musicians are said to be temperamental, and poets can be odd folk at times, but they keep their pettiness out of their art. Our trouble is that as Christian people we have to practice our art all the time. That is the difficulty. But do let us try to show people a religion that is vast and big. Religion is in the same set of ideas as the boundless sea and mighty mountains and agelong purposes and tremendous courage and adventurous faith and broad tolerance and endless good will. Anyone who is on the verge of the Christian community I would ask to pay no attention to the religion of Mrs. Jones, who has stayed away from church for three Sundays because she was not invited to take an urn at a tea meeting, and who, by her absence, is paying back her fellow Christians and showing God what she thinks of him. Pay no attention to Mr. Smith, who has lost his faith in God because the parson didn't hear of his earache in time to visit him before it was better. No! That has nothing to do with religion at all; and neither, I think, have denominational intolerances or pettifogging committee meetings where, as some wit has said, "minutes are kept, but hours are wasted," or where, as a friend of mine once said, "a group of people, composed of those who individually do not intend to do anything, meet together to decide that nothing shall be done."

Let us *magnify* the Lord together! Let us have a *great* God, not one who appears to be a kind of large-sized, elderly gentleman in a black frock coat, who is almost wholly absorbed in our little denominational chapel. No scientist, no poet, no musician, no dramatist, no artist ought to be able to point to a God greater than the Father of Jesus Christ whom we Christians worship. For all science and all poetry and all music and all drama are but revelations of his nature and his ways with men. Our God, vast and infinite, stands behind them all, greater than man's power to imagine, better than man's loveliest thoughts.

So you can relax your body and hush your mind and quiet your heart and rest in the infinity of God. You have heard of the prayer of the Breton fishermen: "O God, help me. My boat is so small. Thy sea is so large." But on that sea the boat can rest, and a million others too, and on the breast of God can rest every troubled spirit in his world.

Look, if you will, at three things that happen if we have a God who is too small.

1. First of all, he is too small for our lives. We have sung the verse that puts this in a nutshell:

> O Lord, how happy should we be
> If we could cast our care on thee,
>   If we from self could rest,
> And feel at heart that one above,
> In perfect wisdom, perfect love,
>   Is working for the best!

There you have the same idea of resting on his infinity. You see, if you have a little God, you almost get into the mood of one who says to him, "I'm afraid you can't do anything to help me." Whereupon, as my teacher and friend Dr. Maltby would have said, God may turn on you and say, "Oh! I dealt with a much harder case than yours yesterday." If there is a God at all. he is big enough to be trusted, and big enough for all our problems and all our needs and all our troubles. "O magnify the Lord with me . . ."

> Behold I will build me a nest on the greatness of God.

> And I smiled to think God's greatness flowed around our
> incompleteness,—
> Round our restlessness, his rest.

2. And if we have a little God, the second thing that happens is that he is too small for our prayers. Here I would say a word hoping that you will not misunderstand. It is right for us to imagine God as our Father. Jesus taught us to do this. He built up his parables on this theme. The least erroneous way of thinking of God at all is to think of him as a perfect Father. But I do want very definitely to say this: We are to think of God as a Father as to his character. We are not to think of him as a Father as to his power or the immense scope of his plans or the strange way those plans *appear* to have of going wrong or looking heartless and cruel. God is a Father in that he will never do anything that is unfatherly, whatever appearances may be. But I am sure our conception of God must go beyond the picture of a good human father. Even in terms of character it is often hard to make the word fit, as we shall see.

For example, people have said to me, "I can't understand how God can listen to my prayers if thousands of other people in other places are praying to him at the same moment." But do you see three snags in such a remark? The questioner is imprisoning God in space and in time and in regard to numbers. I know we are all thus imprisoned. We cannot break out of such a prison. We do not know, therefore, what it is like outside the prison of space and time and calculation. But God does not live in that prison. Even though ten thousand prayers come to him at the same time from Greenland or Australia, it makes no difference to God. We can solve the problem only by telling ourselves—what we cannot hope entirely to comprehend—that a numerical system is only a concession to human thinking. If this were not true, God would be like the old woman who lived in a shoe and "had so many children she didn't know what to do." We've overdone the idea of thinking of him as a Father. We've made him only a bit bigger than ourselves. But even we ourselves realize that the greater the human mind the less bewildering are numbers. To an *infinite* mind numbers are not merely less bewildering, but a nonexistent factor in the working out of the purpose. God does not find it "harder" to guide two lives than one. We might express that simply by saying that numbers do not exist to God in the sense in which they exist for us and imprison us. Or, to put it in yet another way, when you pray, God gives himself in loving attention to you *as if you were the only person in the universe.* The difficulty of the questioner whom I have quoted is that his God is too small. He would find rest for his mind in God's infinity.

I hope that does not sound too abstruse, for actually it has a very practical significance. When you pray for Private Jones who is fighting in Germany, don't imagine that God thinks of him as General Montgomery does. The general, however good, is bound to argue, "Well, I must not mind losing several hundred men if I can win this battle and achieve this end." Being human, he cannot possibly give undivided attention to Private Jones. God is not like that. God's love and care and interest surround Private Jones as if he were the only person in the universe, for God is not limited by our prison of time or space or numbers. Said Augustine, "He loves us every one as though there were but one of us to love." If Private Jones is killed, so far from being "lost," as we say, he lives in another and better room in God's house; and when his little daughter, home in England, is sobbing into her pillow because her daddy is killed, the infinite comfort and love of God are round her life as if hers were the only broken heart in God's care. And if Private Jones's wife says she won't believe in God any more because her man is killed, God doesn't desert her or fail to act purposefully in and through her. Indeed, her power to reject him is itself the power of God, and an infinite God is working out purposes which no mere incident like death can do more than divert into another channel. Let us stop thinking of God as though he were only a very great man, even a good man; for, as he says through his inspired prophet, "My ways are higher than your ways, and my thoughts than your thoughts." His power is far greater than anything we associate with the word "father."

3. If we have too small a God, we shall find also that he is too small for our problems. If you think of God only as a Father, you are picking up a key that will not unlock all the doors because it is so hard to stretch the idea of fatherhood to cover all the things which God allows and does. God is good always, to everybody and forever, but the word "fatherly" makes difficulties.

Let me illustrate in three ways:

a) God appears to allow vast issues to hang on what we call details. A human father doesn't. He doesn't make a university career depend on whether a boy chooses an egg for breakfast or not. Some vast issues in God's plans appear to depend on details. "Had Cleopatra's nose been shorter," said Pascal, "the whole course of the world would have been altered." Do you not imaginatively tremble when you read the story of Mary and Joseph traveling toward Bethlehem? Here is Mary, expecting her child in an hour or two, and riding on a donkey in the dark. Have you ever thought what would have happened if that donkey had stumbled and thrown that rider off? Have you ever thought about your own life and wondered as you noted what immense things appear to hang on some trivial detail? I could give you illustrations from the lives of men and women in which the greatest happenings have appeared to hang on the most trifling events. Truly, big doors swing on small hinges. Sometimes God seems to take tremendous risks, and chance seems to play such a part.

Here is a paragraph from my friend Isaac Foot's recent booklet on Cromwell and Lincoln:

If Cromwell or Lincoln had been born ten years earlier, or ten years later, the likelihood is we should never have heard of either of them. Some would say it was the mere chance of history that when the Civil War, with all its immense consequences to England and the world, broke out in 1642, Oliver Cromwell was there, aged forty-three, in the plentitude of his capacity, and that when Stephen Douglas, in 1854, proposed the repeal of the Missouri Compromise, Abraham Lincoln was there, at the age of forty-five, at the precise moment when he was best fitted to challenge Douglas and all the implications of his policy. These circumstances, *which we might dismiss as mere chance,* were, in fact, accepted by both men as *the mark of a high vocation,* and, rightly or wrongly, they regarded themsleves as instruments prepared and fitted to meet the challenge which they could only ignore at the peril of their souls.

But, you see, when we are talking like this, we are using words that have no meaning to God. With him *there is no such thing as a detail.* He made a fly's leg as carefully as he made a star. The first wasn't a "detail" and the second "important." With him there is no such thing as chance, for the word, even to us, simply covers those happenings which are the product of laws we do not fully understand. If you knew all the laws that operate when you throw up a penny, you would *know* whether it would come down "heads" or "tails." To an infinite God there is no such thing as chance, for nothing is unknown. Indeed, since there is no such thing as time, there is nothing still to happen which can surprise God, for the future and the past stand in the same relationship to God. Both are eternally present. This is hard for us. It raises immense difficulties including the old bogey that if God knows the future man is not free. Yet when we say God knows the past we don't feel that his knowing determined it. Why do we think his knowing the future determines it? The past and future stand in the same relationship to him. Our only mental rest is in the infinity of God, with whom is no detail, no chance, no unimportant event, no past, no present, no future. All exist in his life, which, being infinite, is beyond our comprehension.

b) If you had the power, and you struck a person with lightning, drowned thousands by flood, smote hundreds of thousands by earthquake, you would be locked up in prison, and rightly. As we look at things, we declare that a good father would not allow such a thing to happen if he could prevent it. God, at any rate, *allows* it, and he remains our Father all the time; but I find help by remembering that, while faith must claim for him fatherhood, it must claim for him the infinite purpose acting beyond anything we humans can call fatherly. While we endlessly discuss the problem of pain and suffering, and while there is much light that faith and understanding can throw on such a problem, there is a hard core of impenetrable mystery. I feel it, as you do, when I see a little child suffer. Surely you must see that we need a far bigger conception of God than that he is like a father. We want all that the word "father" can be made to cover, but much more as well.

c) Then, look how unjust life is to many people. A human father tries to be just as he deals with his children. If I took you to Leeds. I could introduce you to two young women. One lived in a happy home, has always had splendid health, went to a very good school, left school and went to Switzerland to "finish," married a nice man, has three lovely children, still lives in a comfortable house, has not suffered through the war, and apparently hasn't a care in the world. But in the same city I could take you to another girl of the same age who lives in a slum. She had an operation, and the surgeon made a mistake. For years she has been in pain and lies in bed in a slum room, from which she can see nothing that God made except a strip of sky. Even that is usually smoke-laden. Further, she isn't a nice pulpit illustration of a person who is always cheerful and bright and into whose room it is a benediction to go. On the contrary, she swears, curses God, and spends hours in bitter, resentful weeping.

But what is God doing to allow such injustice? A human father would put it right if he had the power. And how can that ever be put right? Will the first girl suffer in the next world that the second's troubles may, in some sense, be leveled up? That doesn't make sense, and the second girl doesn't desire it. Can the sufferer have any recompense in another world to make her feel that no injustice has been done? I don't see how. Frankly, I don't know the answer. I don't pretend to know it, and all over the world questions are going up to God from sincere hearts, as well as from bitter, distorted minds—Why? Why? Why? There isn't an answer except that we can rest our minds in the thought of God's infinity. If God is at all, he is infinite. If he is God at all, he is good. For it is incredible that his creatures should be greater than he. Infinite goodness, then, is round about us. We can find peace only in the realization that he must be far greater than our thoughts about him and better than we have the power to conceive. The unquenchable, unsilenceable demand for justice by which we arraign the seeming injustice of God is God's own gift. He planted in our hearts the standards by which we judge him.

I'm not prepared [says a character in a novel by Somerset Maugham] to be made a fool of. If life won't fulfil the demands I make on it, then I have no more use for it. It's a dull and stupid play, and it's only a waste of time to sit it out. I want life to be fair. I want life to be brave and honest. I want men to be decent and things to come right in the end. That's not asking too much, is it? Resignation? That's the refuge of the beaten. Keep your resignation. I don't want it. I'm not willing to accept evil and injustice and ugliness. I'm not willing to stand by while the good are punished and the wicked go scot free. If life means that virtue is trampled on and honesty mocked and beauty fouled, then to hell with life! [2]

Exactly, but what does the last phrase mean? Life has to be *lived*, even though you say, "To hell with it"; and since no explanation is forthcoming which is big enough to fit all the facts, the wise alternative is a faith that rests on God's infinite love and infinite purposefulness.

Let us comfort ourselves by realizing that there are three certainties:

1. We know our values are right—justice, truth, goodness, beauty, kindness, and so on. All who have known God best, assert and exemplify this.

2. We know that our blessedness is his goal; that, in spite of all appearances, he is in charge of the universe, careful of every life; and that we are all within a mighty plan, greater than our conceiving, but the end of which is certainly our highest well-being.

3. We know that our Master, Christ, is a sufficient clue to the nature of God and that in him we can know God as a friend.

Do you realize that when you *know* a person you are content to wait for an explanation of the things he does and allows? "He who hath heard the Word of God," said Ignatius, "can bear his silences."

Some years ago I used an illustration of a little boy whose father

[2] From *The Narrow Corner*. Copyright, 1932, by Doubleday, Doran & Co. Reprinted by permission.

was a surgeon. We imagined somebody going to that boy and saying: "Do you know that your father gets people on a table and,
when they are unconscious and cannot defend themselves, cuts their
bodies with a sharp knife and sometimes takes parts of them away?
How would you like to have that done to you?" The child could
not argue; but if he could, he would rest his mind in the greatness
of his father, *and in his knowledge of his father reached by another
route.* "I know my Daddy," we could imagine the child saying, "and
I have to leave what you say until I can fit the puzzle together."

We cannot comprehend the infinity of God. God will always be
beyond the compass of our little, finite minds, and he will both do
and allow things that puzzle, bewilder, and affright us; but, al-
though we don't know much *about* God, we know God in Jesus and,
knowing, can rest our minds in his infinity.

> Yet, in the maddening maze of things,
> And tossed by storm and flood,
> To one fixed trust my spirit clings;
> I know that God is good! [3]

> I will build me a nest on the greatness of God.

> And I smiled to think God's greatness flowed around our
>   incompleteness,—
> Round our restlessness. his rest.

"O magnify the Lord with me, and let us exalt his name together," for he is greater than all human thought concerning him
and better than all men's dreams.

[3] John Greenleaf Whittier.

A MESSAGE TO THE SPIRITUALLY
DISCOURAGED

I HAVE CHOSEN A NUMBER OF TEXTS BECAUSE I WANT US TO SEE HOW
repeatedly Paul offered this message to the Christians to whom he
wrote:

If any man be in Christ, there is a new creation.
—II Cor. 5:17 (R.V. margin)

Put ye on the Lord Jesus Christ. —Rom. 13:14

As many of you as have been baptized into Christ. have put on Christ.
—Gal. 3:27

Put on the new man. —Eph. 4:24

Ye have put off the old man with his deeds; and have put on the new
man. —Col. 3:9-10

Reckon ye also yourselves to be dead indeed unto sin. but alive unto
God through Jesus Christ our Lord. —Rom. 6:11

Ye are dead, and your life is hid with Christ in God. —Col. 3:3

To all these words of Paul I should like to add the words of
Christ in the parable of the prodigal son:

Bring forth the best robe, and put it on him. —Luke 15:22

Very few of us really know ourselves, and not one of us knows
himself completely. No man has ever seen his own eyes, but only
their reflection, since he uses his eyes with which to see. Similarly,
no man has seen his own spiritual nature, but only its reflection in
his reactions to circumstances. Have you never looked in a mirror
and said, "Good heavens! do I look like that?" Have you never
looked back on the way you behaved in certain circumstances, on

the way you reacted to certain happenings, and said with even deeper dismay, "Good heavens, am I really that kind of person?"

Even that part of our nature at which we *can* look, we see only through colored spectacles. When we try to look at our inner selves, we look at them through spectacles colored by complexes, prejudices, temperamental distortions. influences that affected our childhood, heredity, environment, and so on.

Some people look at themselves through rose-colored spectacles. A man sees himself as "a fairly decent chap," or as a successful businessman, or as a popular speaker. A woman may see herself as a social success, or as a good wife or mother, or perhaps as a beautiful singer. Even those who see themselves in such attractive colors often suspect that deep within the house of their personality are less reputable selves; and sometimes in quiet moments, say of lonely wakefulness, queer forms creep up the cellar steps into the passage, and leer at them in the gloom. But these glimmering ghosts are quickly chased back into the cellar again, and the door is slammed and locked. Such people hate for the phantoms of their unattractive selves to escape from the cellar of the unconscious mind. The cellar is admittedly a better place to keep such ghosts than the living room. But it would be better still to call them all up from the cellar, recognize them, and take steps to throw them out of the house of life forever. The experience called conversion, if genuine, is a good and often a speedy way of driving out devils and giving Christ the key of every room from attic to basement.

I am not going to spend any time talking to those who look at themselves *only* through rose-colored spectacles, because the time would be wasted. Until the spectacles crack and break, such people will probably refuse to be honest with themselves and to see themselves as they are. They can rarely be persuaded that they wear spectacles at all, and no one can help those who say, "There is nothing wrong with me. Nothing is here for treatment or for adjustment. There is no meanness or jealousy, unkindness or resentment, hate or bad temper about me." As Jesus said, with that sad irony of his. "They that be whole need not a physician."

But such people are in the minority. The greater number of people I meet look at themselves through dark lenses. They think the

worst of themselves. They think of themselves as those who count
for little, who are not much good anyway, who have never been
able to make much of a fist of life. The more they know themselves,
the more they tend to despise themselves. Some who have been psy-
choanalyzed feel that they will never be happy again, such depths
of depravity and poisoned motive and dark wells of beastliness have
they found within themselves.

Indeed, an hour of introspection seems to have made even Paul
fall into something like despair about himself, a despair that van-
ishes only when he turns from himself to Christ. Listen to this:

For in me (that is, in my flesh) no good dwells, I know; the wish is there,
but not the power of doing what is right. I cannot be good as I desire to
be, and I do wrong against my wishes. . . . I desire to do what is right,
but wrong is all I can manage; I cordially agree with God's law, so far
as my inner self is concerned, but then I find another law in my members
which conflicts with the law of my mind and makes me a prisoner to sin's
law that resides in my members. . . . Miserable wretch that I am! Who
will rescue me from this body of death? God will! Thanks be to him,
through Jesus Christ our Lord.   —Rom. 7:18-25 (Moffatt)

The phrase Paul uses there, "this body of death," is probably a
reference to that awful method of punishment by which a corpse
was strapped to the back of a criminal so that he had to carry it
about with him wherever he went. He could not remove it. He lay
down with it at night. He rose up with it in the morning. The
stench of its foul corruption was all about him. Even when he sat
down to eat, he could not escape it. The burden must have been
intolerable. Paul uses it as a figure of speech to describe the inescapable burden of sin which man carries, and which he cannot get rid
of by himself. "Who will deliver me," he cries in anguish, "from
this body of death—this awful sense of burden and self-loathing, of
failure and hopelessness?" And then we almost hear the bonds snap-
ping and the horror falling away from him as he says, "God will!
. . . through Jesus Christ our Lord."

Many, I feel, if they were honest and had Paul's gift of self-
expression, would go all the way with him in this description of his
spiritual despair, and yet, perhaps, could not go on with him to

echo his glad, final cry, "God will!" These are the people I should like to help, by getting them to take note of the way in which Paul himself offers encouragement and hope and release to those in the early church who were as heavily burdened as we are.

How can release be obtained? It was to answer this question that I quoted such a rich sample of passages in which Paul says, "Put on Christ." You may possibly feel impatient at those three simple words. The disease is so terrible; the cure sounds so incredibly easy as to be ridiculously ineffective. Here is a man broken by evil, defeated by sin, crushed by its burden; and he goes to this master of the spiritual life, Paul, knowing that he too has passed through these self-same difficulties. He says to Paul, "What *am* I to do?" and Paul simply says, "Put on Christ." It sounds as simple as putting on a robe. Surely it cannot be as easy as that! Surely it means a long, difficult treatment! Surely it demands a tremendous self-discipline over a long period! But no; again and again, to people far worse than ourselves, Paul repeats, "Put on Christ. Put off the old man, put on the new man." Well, this must be looked into! If this is true, it is the most wonderful news in the world.

I heard a little while ago, from a friend who has recently returned from Africa, of an African tribe that used to offer up human sacrifices. In one of their pagan rites the tribesmen demanded that a male member should be selected as the victim who must be put to death. A government official, greatly loved and much admired, did all he knew to stop this practice, but in vain. In desperation, the official finally said, "If you *will* do this, I demand the right to choose the next victim. You will find him tomorrow morning at dawn on the crest of that little hill, robed and veiled. That is the man you must take." The next morning, as the sun came up, the tribesmen looked toward the top of this little knoll, and there stood their victim, robed and veiled. Without any scrutiny, they took him and put him to death. When he was dead, they found that it was their beloved adviser, the government official himself, the man who had pleaded with them to give up their evil ways, and who, finding his words were in vain, had sealed his witness with his life. Is it too imaginative to press that story to our service and suggest that perhaps the robe which that government official wore became for the tribe the symbol of lives that were changed through a noble death?

"Now," says Paul, "put on Christ," as though the nature of Christ were a robe, the robe of one who can still change lives through a noble death, one whose words were beautiful and challenging and healing, but whose words were as nothing compared with the power of a life laid down. "We preach," he said to the Corinthians, "Christ crucified, . . . Christ the power of God, and the wisdom of God."

You may say to me: "Yes, but that's only an illustration, just a figure of speech. To think of the nature of Christ as a robe one can put on may be a beautiful flight of imagination, but it leaves my nature untouched. Underneath the robe I am just the same as I was before."

But wait a minute! Do you believe that Jesus Christ can change a person's life? Ask yourself that question as sincerely as you can. Do you believe that Christianity is a matter of going to church, singing hymns, joining in prayers, listening to sermons, trying to live a good life by the power of your own will; or do you believe that at the heart of Christianity is a tremendous, dynamic, and transforming power, and that Christ can sweep into a man's life and change it utterly? I am going to assume that you believe the latter, for that is the truth of the matter. If it were not, Christianity would not have gone on for so long, would not have achieved the victories which it has achieved on all the shores of the world through two thousand years of time.

If, then, you believe that, let me ask you the next question: When does that change begin? I say *begin* because, admittedly, it may take years to finish completely. But when does it begin? *It begins when you change your mental picture of yourself.* Our great-grandfathers would have said that it begins when you put your faith in Christ. I am expressing the same message rather differently because we live in a different age. But, if you forget everything else in the sermon, try to take hold of this: *It begins when you change your mental picture of yourself.* It begins when you see yourself no longer a man defeated by some secret sin or shuffling along in a state of compromise; as a woman overwhelmed by all her problems, a pitiful, impoverished, weak, defeated person. It begins when you see yourself

to be the kind of person that Christ can make you if he has his way
with you. When Paul says, "Put off the old man," he means put
away the old picture of that broken, defeated prisoner of evil; clean
the slate of the mind of that impression of yourself that shows you
to be defeated, overwhelmed, incapable of being anything different
from what you are now; and see yourself triumphant, victorious,
serene, the master or the mistress of your own life.

I am going to ask you to indulge in an imaginative flight that
may seem fanciful; but if you are in earnest about Christianity,
please do this. Imagine that you are at this moment looking at yourself in a full-length mirror. You are clothed in black, the black of
self-despising and failure and defeat. Then, as you continue to look
in the mirror, Christ, wearing a red robe—and it would be red,
wouldn't it?—comes alongside you, and he puts his red robe right
around you. Now, when you look in the mirror, you are a person
clothed in red; you are a person very close to Christ, and that
blessed union will make you like him. It may take time admittedly;
but already, *already,* you are a changed person, allied with him in
a new closeness of relationship. Something has begun—and I don't
mind how much you emphasize the time it will take to complete
the process—but something has begun which has already made you
a person clothed in red instead of a person clothed in black. His
radiant personality has done something already. In faith that the
old self is dead, its mourning has been covered with resplendent
crimson. You have reckoned yourself dead to sin. You dwell in
Christ. You are one with him. Your life is hid with Christ. You
abide in him. You have put on Christ.

"Bring forth the best robe and put it on him," said the prodigal's
father in the famous story, and *that was done in a moment.* Only
yesterday the prodigal was in the far country among the swine and
the sins; and, if you like to sound a pessimistic note, maybe tomorrow he will have some regrets at what has happened today and
think with evil longing of the delights of the far country. But look,
he is wearing the robe of the son. He is different already. The relationship is different, and he himself knows in his heart that, al-

though yesterday he was not only with the swine but one of them, today he is a son. He has put on the robe.

So it may be with you, my brother, my sister. You are clothed in the black clothes of the spirit. You are downhearted, frustrated, depressed, frightened, defeated, hopeless—one, if not more than one, of these things. And perhaps in your heart you are saying, "It's no good trying. I'm no good. I hate myself, but I shall never be any different. Life is too hard for me. I give it up."

Now, listen to the gospel! Put on Christ! Here is a new nature like a robe put around you by his loving arm. He is offering himself to you. I beseech you, don't shrink away from him. Let that loving arm come round you. Let that scarlet, blood-dyed robe be put over you. And then, above all, *never again look at your old self, wearing the black robe of self-despising, the dark clothes of inescapable failure and unconquerable sin.* "Reckon ye also yourselves to be dead indeed unto sin." "Ye are dead, and your life is hid with Christ in God." Recall the passages at the beginning of the sermon. Listen while Paul exhausts language, weighing the vessels of his words down to the very waterline to make them carry this precious new cargo of the gospel for which no words that were adequate existed. "You are dead," he says; "don't have anything to do with corpses." That old despairing, timid, defeated person, that victim of sin's power, that plaything of hot lust, is dead. All right! Have done with corpses! You are in Christ, and "if any man be in Christ, there is a new creation."

Now please notice two further points: (1) the importance of seeing yourself thus, and (2) the importance of God's seeing you thus.

1. First of all, then, look at the importance of seeing yourself thus. Try to follow this rather carefully, if you will. You cannot be happy unless you can live with yourself. You cannot live with yourself unless, at least to some extent, you like yourself. You cannot like yourself if you know yourself, and the better you know yourself the more you discover within yourself that is hateful, and the less you like yourself. So, as life proceeds, things get worse and worse, because, as you get older, you get to know yourself better, if you are honest, and thus hate yourself more. That explains why so many

elderly people seem so pathetically hungry for the approval of others. The human mind needs appreciation as much as the body needs food and fresh air. Yet elderly people often find themselves out, and then begin to hate themselves secretly. The reason why they hunger for approval is that the approval of others is an anodyne to deaden the pain of hating themselves. They want others to bolster them up, to tell them they're not such bad folk after all. The approval of others counteracts to some extent their disapproval of themselves. But here, as in every dilemma of the human mind, the Christian gospel comes with its complete answer. Thus the only way to be independent of the approval of others is to approve of yourself; and since he who knows himself can never approve of himself, your peace of mind depends on changing yourself; and your only hope of doing that is found in Christ. In Christ—or, to keep the figure, by putting on the robe, by putting on Christ—you can exchange the self you hate for the new self he is creating; and you are to see yourself *already* as the kind of person you will certainly become, unless you throw off the robe and turn your back on him.

But see the importance of looking upon yourself thus in another way. We all love to be loved, and when things are not going well with us, we all love to get sympathy. But let me indicate one danger to those who, almost morbidly, demand sympathy from others. If you go about asking for sympathy, you are etching deeper into the mind the picture of yourself as a person *needing* sympathy, that is, a weak person. Those who have been deprived of love, and whose nature is emotionally starved, tend quite naturally either to indulge in self-pity or to demand a great deal of sympathy from others, or both; for both are love substitutes, and we want at all costs to be loved. But it would be healthier if, while we admitted our longing for the love of our fellow men and women, we refused to allow ourselves to live with a mental picture of ourselves that showed us to be the kind of people who *depended* on others. The line of the hymn, "Thou, O Christ, art all I want," is literally true, though it may take years for us to realize it; and to "put on Christ" means holding in our own minds a picture of ourselves as already the resplendent, scarlet-cloaked beings, the new men in Christ, which we are becoming in him. Then, instead of needing sympathy, you be-

come the kind of person who offers it to others; instead of showing
a pitiful dependence on being loved, you go about among your fel-
lows as one who offers love; and, strangely enough—because this is
how God has arranged life—love comes back to the person who
gives it in a far greater measure than it comes to the man or woman
who demands it. There is a very sound psychology, as well as a deep
piety, behind the ancient prayer that says: "Teach us, O Lord, not
to seek so much to be consoled as to console, not so much to be
understood as to understand, not so much to be loved as to love.
Show us that it is in giving that we receive, in self-forgetting that
we find, in dying that we waken to eternal life."

Seeking always for sympathy has another bad effect on the soul;
it undermines courage. It is easier to put the healing ointment of
sympathy on the sore place than to find out why it becomes so sore.
The reason is often a fear that must be rooted out or overcome. We
tend to accept sympathy instead of facing the fear that makes us
want sympathy. The more we can switch attention from the symp-
tom of weakness to the action that will overcome it, the better. The
sympathy of others is very lovely, and we are entitled to a measure
of it as long as it does not become an anodyne for our own cowardice and for the pain which the recognition of our cowardice would
inflict upon us. To "put on Christ" means identifying ourselves
with one who will take us, cowards though we are, and change our
nature so that we shan't need sympathy, but become the kind of
people who can give it. In him we shall assess courage higher than
the need of sympathy. Emphasis on the latter makes us perma-
nently weak characters. To see ourselves as courageous "in Christ"
makes the beginning of strength, the strength of those who can
"stand their corner" and cope with their difficulties and say with
Paul, "In him who strengthens me, I am able for anything" (Moffatt). As the new picture of ourselves "in Christ" grows stronger and
clearer in our own minds, we tend to become like it and enjoy the
power it brings more than we used to enjoy the sympathy of others
concerning our weakness. It is better to be "on top of things," as we
say, with that exhilarating feeling of conquest, than underneath
them, however sympathetic people may be with us in our adver-
sities.

2. Second, turn to the importance of God's seeing us as new men in Christ. You will remember that poem of Tennyson called "The Ancient Sage," where, talking about faith, he says:

> She spies the summer through the winter bud,
> She tastes the fruit before the blossom falls,
> She hears the lark within the songless egg,
> She finds the fountain where they wail'd "Mirage."

That is how God looks at you. Remember that God is not imprisoned in time. You can see yourself only as you are now, and you feel that years and years of hard climbing stretch before you. But I am sure it is true to say that God's assessment of your character is not in terms of present achievement, but of tendency and direction. God, from beyond the time prison, can see you as already perfected, can see you as you are bound to become unless you creep out from under that robe—the robe of Christ's nature—and cut yourself off from its power. And, frankly, God can receive you—since he is utterly righteous and perfectly holy—not as you are in yourself now, for in you is no worth at all, but only as you are in Christ. Man has worth only in what he is capable of becoming, and he is capable of becoming his maximum only through Christ. If I may coin a word, man's "worthness" is established, not in any value he can attain by his own efforts, merit, or abilities, but because of what Christ can make of him. That which he of himself could never become, and that which men would deny as being of any value, is worth a lot to the God who sees him in Christ—a Christ who thought man was worth dying for. As Browning says,

> All I could never be,
> All men ignored in me,
> This I was worth to God.

Thus, in a beautiful Communion hymn, we pray that God will "only look on us as found in him."

I charge you, then, to make this day the day of your conversion. Many of us have never been converted. We have been brought up in Christian homes, but, to be quite honest, we have been content with a conventional sham. The transforming power of Christ has never been released into our lives. We sing the hymns and say the words, but they are forms without the fire. If you doubt this, ask yourself two or three questions of great significance. Could you lead another to Jesus Christ? Have you found something in him that you could pass on? If the early Christians had been like you, do you think Christianity would have spread through the pagan world? We are shy of the very word "conversion." We think it has something to do with emotional excitement, with revivalistic meetings that nice, respectable, cultured, well-educated people despise. But conversion, which of course *may* be a highly emotional experience, has much more to do with a simple act of obedience and with a simple turning toward Christ in some quiet hour of the soul's revelation of its own most desperate need. Don't wait for some great dramatic event or emotional experience. Christ offers himself to you. Take him in faith. Don't bother about your feelings. Indeed, you may *feel* no different right away. But "put on Christ." Make a beginning with him and reaffirm that dear allegiance every morning. Alter your mental picture of yourself, and see yourself, by his grace, as already the changed personality which deep in your heart you desire to be.

But I must give you some warnings:

1. You will often want to slip back and be the "old man" you used to be. That "old man" is an old friend, and it is easier to live with old friends than with new friends. Christ, the new friend, will make new demands, set up new conflicts, bring new challenges. For that reason, many in the early days of Christian discipleship find life much harder and less happy. There was no conflict before, no challenge. They pursued the path of their own will. Now they are pulled up at nearly every step. But if you slip out from under the robe, slip back again; and if you fall and put off Christ, then put on Christ again every evening.

2. The devil will try to tempt you that nothing has happened at all, that all is just imaginative talk. Well, recall that the triumphant history of the Christian church through years of persecution and the history of the church that is being written now—where in India and China and Africa men are finding in these old New Testament

words the very power of God—adequately answer that argument. Why shouldn't it all be true for you?

3. You will hesitate to believe that your personality is being changed, and like a frightened horse you will tremble and shy at the dangers in the road. I would say to you, "Never mind if you do tremble! Put this newly seen, newborn personality to the test. If you believe in yourself, you will find that the new self is stronger than the old, for Christ's personality is now added to yours; and if you feel like trembling, well, tremble!" Do you remember that lovely story of Turenne, the beloved marshal of France, who sacrificed so much that he might maintain his Christian Protestant witness? When he was shaving just before a battle, his hand trembled violently, and he turned on his own body and said, "Tremblest thou, vile carcass? Thou wouldst tremble more if thou knewest where I am going to take thee this day." But though he trembled, he went on. I tremble too, grow sick with feelings of fear, feel my heart turn to lead within my breast. But when I have had the courage to put "the new man" to the test, Christ has never let me down.

4. Remember, lastly, that often when you don't feel any different, and when you feel a failure, neither God nor others see you thus. How well I remember in Leeds a man coming into my vestry and giving me a contribution for the poor because his daughter's life had been changed in a service that I had conducted. He said that the whole atmosphere of the home was different. Yet, five minutes earlier, the girl herself had been talking to me in great depression and almost in tears because she felt such a failure and because, though she sought to follow Christ, she found her home life overwhelmingly hard and thought her witness a failure.

In my study a week or two ago a ministerial friend told me this lovely story. He said that, when he was a little boy, he was out for a walk with his father, and they saw a most vivid rainbow, the end of which lighted up the rocks quite near the path along which they were walking. The little boy said to his father, "Daddy, let me go and stand in the light of the rainbow," and off he went. Of course to the boy the light of the rainbow was always a little bit farther on and never seemed to bathe him in its splendor. But when his father looked at his dear son, the glory of the rainbow light seemed to transfigure him. When we set ourselves to leave the paths of selfishness along which we have been walking and seek to enter into spiritual realities, the light of the glory of God seldom seems to be round about us. It always seems a little farther on. Sometimes we grow disheartened and depressed. Achievement falls so short of desire. But I think when our heavenly Father looks upon us he sees the light of spiritual beauty around us, because the glory of Christ transfigures a man immediately as he steps off the path of selfish desire and longs to be caught up into the light and life of God. You may not discern the light around you, but God sees it, and, more often than we think, other people do too.

Lift up your hearts, then, and take courage, for the man who "puts on Christ" has nothing to fear in this life or the next. Claim your inheritance as a child of God. Realize yourself united with Christ and, remembering that Christ is God and that you are linked with him, remember that there is no power of evil which can defeat God, nor anything that can possibly happen in this world or another that can overwhelm the man who is one with God in Christ. That is what made John Wesley translate the poem of Zinzendorf thus:

> Jesus, thy blood and righteousness
> My beauty are, my glorious dress;
> 'Midst flaming worlds, in these arrayed,
> With joy shall I lift up my head.

> Bold shall I stand in thy great day,
> For who aught to my charge shall lay?
> Fully absolved through these I am,
> From sin and fear, from guilt and shame.

> .   .   .   .   .   .

> O let the dead now hear thy voice,
> Now bid thy banished ones rejoice,
> Their beauty this, their glorious dress,
> Jesus, thy blood and righteousness!

Put on Christ! Do it now, as though just you and Christ were alone in a vast solitude. Bow before him in adoration and worship until you feel the robe of his loving nature put around you, and realize that it is you, worthless in yourself, that he thought worth dying for, and will never leave until he has made you all his own. All life can be different for you. Don't let anything put you off this great transaction. "If *any man* be in Christ, there is a new creation." Why not you?

This is the end of this publication.

Any remaining blank pages are for our book binding requirements and are blank on purpose.

To search thousands of interesting publications like this one, please remember to visit our website at:

http://www.kessinger.net

CPSIA information can be obtained at www.ICGtesting.com
Printed in the USA
BVOW011431300112

281727BV00011B/120/P